CRIMINAL BRITAIN

CRIMINAL BRITAIN

A PHOTOGRAPHIC HISTORY OF THE COUNTRY'S MOST NOTORIOUS CRIMES

mirrorpix

The
History
Press

First published 2019

The History Press
The Mill, Brimscombe Port
Stroud, Gloucestershire, GL5 2QG
www.thehistorypress.co.uk

British Library Cataloguing in Publication Data.
A catalogue record for this book is available from the British Library.

ISBN 978 0 7509 9074 5

Typesetting and origination by The History Press
Printed in Turkey by Imak

INTRODUCTION

BY SIMON FARQUHAR

Britain has not yet, and perhaps never will, permit the televising of trials. Instead, the public must rely on the quaint tradition of courtroom sketches and newspaper reports, the one realm of crime journalism that has remained unchanged over the last century. When it comes to crime scenes, criminals and police procedure, however, our media is now being allowed increasingly intimate coverage. We live in an age in which documentaries and news reports can offer us CCTV footage of a murderer leaving the scene of his crime, bodycam footage of his arrest and recordings of his interrogation and confession. The motivation for allowing such materials into the public domain has not been to feed our insatiable fascination with criminality, but to help us to acknowledge the necessity and unpleasantness of police work. Because what criminals – and in particular, what *murderers* do – is often unthinkable and frequently unimaginable. Allowing the public a closer look at what close contact with evil people actually entails has allowed the return of a certain amount of respect for those whose business it is to keep us safe and to bring those who harm us to justice.

For most of the past century, however, it was the work of the press photographer that got us as close to real crime as most of us would ever wish to get.

The haunting quality of these pictures partly lies in what they leave to our worried imaginations. A crime scene with the victim covered up. The front of a house that holds dreadful secrets within. The face of a serial killer. None of us will ever know the voices of Dr Crippen, John Reginald Christie or John George Haigh. Instead we gaze at their photographs in the same way that we gaze at mannequins in the Chamber of Horrors, searching in vain for a hint of evil in their seemingly ordinary and unremarkable faces.

When researching my book *A Dangerous Place: The Story of the Railway Murders*, I realised that a crime committed against one person has countless victims. Unlike crime fiction, the reality of murder rarely involves intricate plotting and fathomable motives. Instead, murder is usually senseless and sporadic, its detection leaving us with more questions than answers. Even if justice is done, it does nothing to quell the pain that has been unleashed. In time, the journalists and the photographers move on. Families are left to find ways not to get over their pain, but to learn to live with it.

But some crimes live on in the public consciousness. These pictures are the bleak souvenirs of some of those crimes.

Perhaps our fascination with crime is a way of subtly instructing ourselves that we must be vigilant in this frightening world. If that is so, we should perhaps consider a more positive message when immersing ourselves in such stories. Like another persistently popular genre of history – namely that of war – crime is about cruelty, injustice and tragedy. But there is also courage: the courage of witnesses, the courage of survivors, and the courage and endeavour of those whose job it is to detect such crimes.

As we educate ourselves on the cruelty of a small number of people, we should also remind ourselves that at a murder trial, there is usually only one person in that packed courtroom who is accused of wrongdoing: a simple illustration of the fact that not only are evil people few, they are always outnumbered by the valiant.

SERIAL KILLERS

⋀ Durward Street (then called Bucks Row) in Whitechapel, London, as seen in 1965 before the street was largely demolished. This was the murder scene of 41-year-old Mary Ann Nichols, a prostitute who was Jack the Ripper's first victim.

◄ The front of 29 Hanbury Street in 1965, the murder scene of Annie Chapman, Jack's second victim, in Whitechapel on 8 September 1888. This has since been demolished.

➤ The back yard of 29 Hanbury Street, where the body of Annie Chapman was discovered.

◄▲ Catherine Eddowes, Jack's fourth victim, was found here in Mitre Square, Whitechapel. These images show Mitre Square as it looked in 1965.

▾➤ John Christie is led away by police after being charged with multiple murders.

◄ The Rillington Place murderer, John Christie, pictured here with his wife Ethel.

➤ A macabre scene as police dig for bodies at 10 Rillington Place.

▲ Crowds gather outside 10 Rillington Place, Notting Hill, as police remove furniture for forensic examination and dig in the garden looking for further victims of John Christie.

▶ 79 Gloucester Road in Kensington, where the bodies of Mr and Mrs McSwan and their son were found in the basement, having been murdered by the Acid Bath murderer, John George Haigh.

▲▶ Members of the general public look over the fence as detectives search for remains and clues in the grounds of the Hurstlea Products factory at Crawley, the scene of the Acid Bath murders.

▲ John Haigh, driving away from his residence in Onslow Court Hotel, Kensington, following the disappearance of wealthy widow Mrs Olive Durand-Deacon. He was later convicted of her murder.

▲ Crowds gather outside 79 Gloucester Road in March 1949 where detectives investigate the disappearance of Olive Durand-Deacon, John Haigh's last victim.

◄▲ Police dig Saddleworth Moor in October 1965, looking for the victims of the Moors Murderers, Ian Brady and Myra Hindley.

▲ Police continue to search for the bodies of the Moors Murderers.

▲ Anne Downey, mother of Lesley Ann Downey, stands near searchers as they search for her daughter, victim of the Moors Murderers.

▲ Lesley Ann Downey's uncle is restrained by police as Ian Brady and Myra Hindley leave Hyde Court.

◄ An angry crowd greets Ian Brady and Myra Hindley outside Hyde Court, Manchester, on 28 October 1965.

➤ Ian Brady being taken away in a police car in May 1966.

▲ Detectives Jim Butterworth (left) and Sergeant John Mackrill walk the Bradford alley where Barbara Leach was murdered by the Yorkshire Ripper, Peter Sutcliffe.

▲ Police play a tape supposedly of the Ripper to Bingo players in Bradford on 21 September 1979.

◄ A lynch mob gathers outside Dewsbury police station, where Peter Sutcliffe has been arrested for murder.

▲ Detectives and pathologists in Savile Park, Halifax, where the body of Josephine Whitaker, a victim of Peter Sutcliffe, was found on 5 April 1979.

➤ A handcuffed Peter Sutcliffe is led away from court.

◄ Forensic police search the garden of 23 Cranley Gardens, home of serial killer Dennis Nilsen, for more remains.

▲ Douglas Stewart, a survivor of Dennis Nilsen, stands outside the Golden Lion pub in Soho, where Nilsen met several of his victims.

▲ The bathroom at Dennis Nilsen's Muswell Hill flat where he butchered and dismembered the bodies of his victims.

▲ The tie used by Dennis Nilsen to strangle his victims.

➤ Dennis Nilsen being led away by police.

∧ Fingerpost Field, near Much Marcle in Herefordshire, where the body of Anne McFall, one of Fred West's early victims, was found fifty-six days after police began the search for her.

◄ A policeman carrying a box from the home of serial killers Rosemary and Fred West as they search their home at 25 Cromwell Street, Gloucester, in March 1994.

▲➤ The basement of 25 Cromwell Street.

∧ Police stand guard outside 25 Cromwell Street in April 1994.

▲ Dr Harold Shipman's surgery in Hyde.

▲ Harold Shipman arrives for questioning at Ashton-under-Lyne police station in September 1998.

SHOCKING CRIMES

⋏ Dr Hawley Crippen is extradited back to Britain from Canada in August 1910 following the murder of his wife.

◄ Dr Crippen and Ethel Neave, Crippen's accomplice and lover, in the dock at the Old Bailey in October 1910.

▲ Crowds gather outside Bow Street courts, waiting to see witnesses for the trial of George Joseph Smith, on 30 March 1915.

◄ The Brides in the Bath murderer, George Joseph Smith, watches from the dock at Bow Street in February 1915.

▲ Police officers searching the woods at Fairley Hill in 1952, where Linda Bowyer was found strangled by John Straffen.

◄ From left to right: Mrs Alice Simms, mother of Linda Bowyer; Mrs D. Pullen, foster mother of Brenda Goddard; and Mrs Batstone, mother of Cecily Batstone – all mothers of children murdered by John Straffen in 1952.

➤ Ruth Ellis (right) standing next to David Blakely, for whose murder she became the last woman to be hanged in Britain.

◀ The crowd outside Wandsworth Prison in January 1953, awaiting the execution of Ruth Ellis.

▲ Michael Gregsten's Morris Minor is found in Barkingside, Essex, on 23 August 1961. Gregsten was shot and killed by James Hanratty, the A6 murderer.

▲ John Lennon and Yoko Ono protesting against James Hanratty's execution at the charity world premiere of *The Magic Christian* at the Kensington Odeon on 11 December 1969.

▲ 46 Lower Belgrave Street, London, SW1: the home of Lord Lucan. A photograph taken on 16 June 1975, the day of the inquest into the murder of Sandra Rivett, the nanny to Lucan's children.

▲ Lady Lucan leaving the Westminster Coroners Court following the inquest into the death of Sandra Rivett.

> Jeremy Bamber arrives at Maldon Magistrates Court following his arrest.

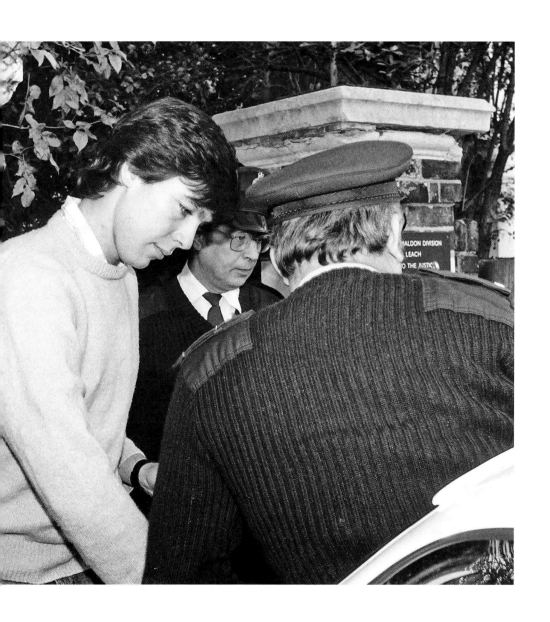

▲ White House Farm at Tolleshunt D'Arcy, Essex, where Jeremy Bamber murdered five members of his adoptive family.

▲ John Bassett, the detective in charge of the Rachel Nickell murder enquiry, at Wimbledon Common, the scene of her murder in 1992.

▲ Robert Napper arrives at court, where he was convicted of the manslaughter of Rachel Nickell on the grounds of diminished responsibility.

▲ Floral tributes for James Bulger on the day of his funeral, 1 March 1993.

◀ Police search the site where murdered toddler James Bulger was found in February 1993.

◄ The family of Stephen Lawrence – his mother Doreen, his father Neville and his brother Stuart – speak to the press outside the Old Bailey on 3 January 2012, following the conviction of Gary Dobson and David Norris for his murder.

▲ Flowers and tributes are left on Stephen Lawrence's memorial stone in Eltham, London, following the convictions of Dobson and Norris. It took almost nine years for the men to face justice.

◄▲ Police guard the entrance to Itsu restaurant in London's Piccadilly on 27 November 2006. Former spy Alexander Litvinenko had met with a contact at the restaurant prior to falling ill and succumbing to polonium poisoning.

▲ Police examine a car believed to belong to murdered architect Joanna Yeates' landlord Chris Jefferies, who was arrested, questioned and bailed by police in connection with her murder. Jefferies was later released without charge.

▲ A floral tribute at Longwood Lane, near Bristol, where Joanna Yeates' body was found on Christmas Day 2010.

GANGLAND

▲ The scene inside the Blind Beggar pub on Whitechapel Road, London, where Richardson gang associate George Cornell was shot dead by Ronnie Kray on 9 March 1966.

▲ The house in Evering Road, North London, where Reggie Kray murdered Jack 'The Hat' McVitie on 29 October 1967.

➤ The Kray brothers (left to right: Reggie, Charlie, Ronnie) outside their family's house in Valance Road, London's East End.

▲ The Kray twins following their sentencing at the Old Bailey.

➤ Charlie Kray outside the Old Bailey.

▲ The team who caught the Krays. From left to right: Detective Daphne Robeson, Detective Carole Liston, Detective Janet Adams, Sergeant A. Gallacher, Sergeant A. Trevette, Commander John du Rose, Superintendent Leonard Nipper Read, Inspector Frank Cater, Superintendent Henry Mooney and Sergeant Algernon Hemmingway.

INFAMOUS HEISTS

▲ Police examine Sears Crossing in Buckinghamshire, the scene of the Great Train Robbery, in August 1963.

◄ Police examine the train that had been commandeered during the Great Train Robbery.

◄ Ronnie Biggs attending a hearing at Aylesbury Crown Court on 4 October 1963.

▲ Charles Wilson, Great Train Robber, being led away, handcuffed to a prison officer, from Aylesbury Crown Court on 10 September 1963.

◄ Bruce Reynolds, the mastermind of the Great Train Robbery, under arrest in November 1968.

▲ Police stop, search and question potential witnesses at scene of the Brink's-Mat gold bullion robbery.

◀ The scene of the Brink's-Mat robbery, which occurred on 26 November 1983.

∧ Gordon Parry is arrested by police in 1990, on suspicion of laundering money that was connected to the Brink's-Mat robbery.

▲ John Fleming, wanted in connection with the Brink's-Mat robbery, arriving with police at Heathrow airport.

▲ Police at the scene of the Hatton Garden robbery in London, April 2015.

▲ The hole cut in a tile at the front door to Hatton Garden Safe Deposit Ltd, where it is believed work was being undertaken on a new security system at the time of the heist.

◄ The entrance to the rear of Hatton Garden Safe Deposit Ltd.

◄▲ Police raid an address in Dartford, Kent, that belongs to Hatton Garden robbery mastermind Brian Reader.

▲ Hugh Doyle leaves Woolwich Crown Court on bail, having been accused of helping to dispose of the jewellery and other items stolen in the Hatton Garden robbery.

KILLING SPREES

⋏ Gunman Barry Williams killed four people and seriously wounded four others after opening fire in West Bromwich and Nuneaton on 26 October 1978.

➤ Barry Williams arrives at West Bromwich Magistrates Court on 28 October 1978.

▲ Residents of Andrew Road in the aftermath of Barry William's shooting spree.

▲ The remains of Michael Ryan's house in South View, Hungerford. Ryan had set fire to it before embarking on a killing spree in August 1987.

▲ Police in action during the gun siege in Hungerford, in which Michael Ryan killed sixteen people.

➤ Police keeping guard outside John O'Gaunt School, where Michael Ryan committed suicide following the Hungerford Massacre.

▲▼ Police attend a press conference in Hungerford.

➤ Police examine a car outside John O'Gaunt School.

◄ The sign at Dunblane Primary School, the scene of gunman Thomas Hamilton's killing spree on 13 March 1996.

▼ Police stand guard outside Hamilton's house in Dunblane.

▲ Politicians arrive with wreaths at Dunblane Primary School.

◄ Mourners pay their respects and leave tributes at the scenes of the killings by Derrick Bird in several Cumbrian villages.

▲ Tributes left outside a house in Cumbria, one of the scenes of Bird's killings.

TERRORISM

⌃ The aftermath of an IRA bomb blast at the Old Bailey in London in 1973.

◄ The Birmingham pub bombings took place on 21 November 1974 and were attributed to the Provisional IRA. The devices were placed in two central Birmingham pubs: the Mulberry Bush and the Tavern in the Town; 21 people were killed and 182 injured.

➤ A police officer stands guard over the wreckage of one of the Birmingham pubs.

➤ The aftermath of an IRA bomb at Walton's restaurant in Chelsea in November 1975.

▲ Policemen examine the wreckage outside Scott's restaurant after the IRA threw a bomb through the window in November 1975.

➤ Damage to the Grand Hotel in Brighton following an IRA bomb explosion. Prime Minister Margaret Thatcher and her cabinet were staying there during the 1984 Conservative Party Conference.

⋀◀ Police examine the wreckage of the Pam Am 747 jumbo jet that crashed in Lockerbie on 21 December 1988 after a bomb exploded onboard.

◄ The crater caused by the plane crash.

▲➤ Damage to local buildings caused by the Lockerbie plane crash.

▲ A policewoman pays her respect to the victim of the IRA's Victoria station bomb in February 1991.

▲ Forensics search the scene of the IRA's Warrington bomb attack, which killed two children and injured dozens more on 20 March 1993.

◀ The 1996 Manchester IRA bombing caused extensive damage to nearby buildings but fortunately led to no fatalities.

▲ Two people died and dozens were injured when a nail bomb ripped through the Admiral Duncan, one of Soho's oldest gay pubs, in April 1999. The perpetrator, a Neo-Nazi named David Copeland, was later convicted of carrying out a hate crime.

◄ The aftermath of the 1998 Omagh car bomb in Northern Ireland, which killed twenty-nine people.

➤ Four radical Islamic suicide bombers killed 52 people on London's busy transport network on 7 July 2007.

▲ What was left of the number 10 to Hackney Wick after it was blown up as part of the 7/7 bombings.

▲ Police on Westminster Bridge, London, following the terror attack carried out by Khalid Masood on 22 March 2017.

▲ A chilling look into the abandoned Bunch of Grapes bar at London Bridge, following the terror attack on 3 June 2017.

▲ A defiant message left among the flowers and cards after the Finsbury Park Mosque terror attack on 19 June 2017.

Temp: 17°C   13:58   23/05/17

WE ♥ MCR

G M Police Emergency Number
0161 856 9400

a terror attack

MANCHESTER CITY COUNCIL

▲ A message of hope amidst police presence following the terror attack on Manchester Arena that claimed the lives of twenty-two young concertgoers and injured hundreds more.